THE
HOMELESS

BY
Laurie Beckelman

EDITED BY
Anita Larsen

CONSULTANT
Elaine Wynne, M.A., Licensed Psychologist

New York

CIP
LIBRARY OF CONGRESS CATALOGING IN PUBLICATION DATA

Beckelman, Laurie
  The homeless

(The facts about)
Includes index.
SUMMARY: Discusses the problems of and services available to the homeless in large cities and small communities, the rising number of homeless families, myths and stereotypes about homeless people, and ways to help the homeless.
  1. Homelessness — United States — Juvenile literature. 2. Homeless persons — United States — Juvenile literature. [1. Homelessness. 2. Homeless persons.] I. Larsen, Anita. II. Title. III. Series.
HV4505.B44   1989   362.5'8'0973—dc 20   89-1432
ISBN 0-89686-439-1

PHOTO CREDITS

Cover: Third Coast Stock Source: Paul H. Henning
Third Coast Stock Source: (D & I MacDonald) 4; (Ralf-Finn
    Hestoff) 20; (Jeff Lowe) 26, 29
FPG International: (O'Brien and Mayor) 8, 30, 40
DRK Photo: (C. C. Lockwood) 10
The Image Works (Bob Daemmrich) 13, 23; (Larry Kolvoord) 14;
Journalism Services: (Joseph Jacobson) 35

Macmillan Publishing Company
866 Third Avenue
New York, NY 10022
Collier Macmillan Canada, Inc.

CRESTWOOD HOUSE

Produced by Carnival Enterprises
Printed in the United States of America
First Edition
10 9 8 7 6 5 4 3 2 1

TABLE OF CONTENTS

important questions. Knowing the answers to them is important, too.

WHAT DO YOU KNOW ABOUT HOMELESS PEOPLE?

Many people have false ideas about the homeless. They think all homeless people are bums. They think people are homeless because they want to be or because they don't try hard enough. None of this is true. But these ideas keep people from helping.

How much do you know about the homeless? Take this true/false quiz. The answers to some of the questions might surprise you.

1. All homeless people are crazy or drunk.

False.

An alcoholic rummaging through a garbage pail and a "bag lady" muttering to herself are common sights on city streets. These unfortunate people have health problems. They suffer from an *addiction* to alcohol or drugs or some form of *mental illness*. Alcohol and drug addiction and mental illnesses are diseases. When people with these diseases don't get medical help, they are often unable to keep their jobs or care for themselves. Many end up homeless.

Homeless people are not all alcoholic or mentally ill.

But not all homeless people are alcoholic or mentally ill. In 1987, the U.S. Conference of Mayors took a survey of, or studied, 26 cities. The survey found that a little over half of the homeless living in cities have these problems. The number may be lower in other parts of the country.

Who are the rest of the homeless? They are men and women who lost their jobs and then their homes because they couldn't pay the rent or mortgage (monthly payments to a bank). They are families. They are teenagers who have run away from home. They are retired

can never say, "I'd rather have ham and cheese today." You can never buy a candy bar for dessert.

At night you return to the shelter. You can never invite a friend over to visit. You can never switch the television channel because 20 or 30 other people are watching with you. Yet you know you're lucky. At least you have shelter.

Now imagine it is 20 degrees outside. The snow is ankle deep. You are wearing the three sweaters and one warm coat that you own, but you still shiver. You have not had a hot meal all day. It is night. The public library where you have spent the past three hours is closed. You walk along the streets of your city, hands thrust deep in your pockets. You search for a McDonald's. Maybe a hurried diner has left some warm French fries. If you can find some food, you think, you can face the night. You can face the abandoned building where you sleep on a mattress made of newspapers. Your blanket is a cardboard box.

These two examples are typical of what it's like to be homeless. Is it true that homeless people get a free ride? You decide.

HOMELESS AROUND THE WORLD

People are homeless all over the world. The World Health Organization estimated in 1987 that there were

When a soup kitchen is not available, homeless people search for food wherever they can find it.

100 million homeless people on Earth. If this many people held hands, they could circle the globe five times.

These people are homeless for many reasons. Sometimes disasters like earthquakes or floods destroy people's homes. Sometimes wars cause people to flee their homes. They are *refugees*, people who go to another country to escape danger. They often live in tents or shacks in temporary camps. They no longer have permanent homes.

Simar is a refugee. She was an infant when her family fled their native Afghanistan in 1980. They left behind a farm—and the Soviet soldiers who brought war to their village. They went to Pakistan, to a camp of tents and mud houses. It is the only home Simar has known. She and her family are not alone. Almost three million Afghans live in refugee camps in Pakistan. Almost half are children like Simar.

Each night, Simar's mother tells her about the home they left in Afghanistan. She speaks of vines heavy with grapes, of fields ripe with wheat. She says they will return someday. To Simar, it sounds like a fairy tale.

Simar's family fled a war. Other refugees flee famine. They leave a land where crops will not grow and animals and people die of starvation. They go to other countries or to cities in their own countries. They search for jobs, so they can buy food and shelter for their families.

In the Sudan, the largest country in Africa, some of

these refugees are boys as young as five years old. They leave the drought and famine that have struck their villages for Khartoum, the capital city. Girls are forbidden to leave home.

Twelve-year-old Ali is one of Khartoum's 10,000 street children. To reach the city, he rode for four days on the roof of a train across the desert. On the way, he dreamed of the candy stand he would open in Khartoum.

But Khartoum offered few chances to earn money for Ali. Living day to day was hard enough. Ali got his food from restaurant garbage cans. He got his money by begging and picking pockets. He slept with his new "family"—four boys like himself—on the sandy streets of the city. After two months in the city, he was still hungry and ragged. His dream of a candy stand was gone.

Poor people worldwide leave their homes in the country for the city. Not all of them are starving. Many are simply searching for a better life. Juan was one such *migrant*.

Juan headed for Mexico City when he was eighteen. Like many migrants, he moved in with relatives. Juan's uncle, aunt, and three cousins lived in a one-room apartment in a *barrio*. That's a crowded slum on the edge of the city. Juan didn't plan to stay long. He thought he would soon earn enough money for his own room. He wanted to start a family.

But Juan had little education and few job skills. The

odd jobs he could find paid poorly. He could barely make ends meet. When he did marry and move, it wasn't to an apartment. He built a shack with branches and cardboard and scraps of metal. His shack had no electricity and no running water for a toilet or shower. A house like Juan's is not really a home. It does little to protect health or provide warmth and security.

Like many refugees and migrants, Juan never found the better life.

HOMELESS IN AMERICA

Do the things that make people homeless around the world explain homelessness in America? Not really.

We do have earthquakes and floods. We have blizzards and hurricanes. We even have had a volcano erupt. But we are a very lucky country. Similar tragedies in other parts of the world have left tens of thousands homeless. In recent years, such disasters have affected fewer people here. We recover quickly from such disasters, too. Our country is rich. The government and relief groups help people rebuild their homes or find new ones.

Refugee problems don't explain why Americans are homeless, either. America has welcomed many people who have fled political violence or economic hardship in their own countries. Earlier in this century, many came from Italy, Ireland, and Eastern Europe. More recently, people have come from Central or South America and Southeast Asia. America has the fourth largest refugee population in the world. But most of America's homeless are not from foreign countries. They are Americans. They were born here and have grown up in this country.

Nor do most of America's homeless go to cities in search of food or jobs. Most homeless Americans have been long-time residents of the areas in which they live. Only a few move to new cities to look for jobs. And we don't have famine in this country. Food is plentiful everywhere in America. People are not forced to leave an area where food is scarce in search of plenty.

But people are hungry in America despite supermarkets brimming with food. They are homeless even though our country is one of the richest in the world. What's going on?

Homelessness is not a new problem for our country. In the 1930s, *shantytowns* sprang up in vacant lots all across the nation. Shantytowns are villages of makeshift houses. They were home to people who had lost their jobs and houses during the Great Depression, which began after the Crash of 1929. Factories and mines closed. Businesses and banks failed.

By 1932, one out of every four American adults was unemployed. In the mid-1930s, drought turned vast areas of fertile farmland in the Great Plains states into a "dust bowl." The land became so dry nothing could grow. Farms failed. Tens of thousands of farmers and their families moved west to look for work. The nation faced the worst economic crisis of its history.

That is not the case today. We are not in a depression. Quite the opposite. Since the early 1980s, the number of people at work in America has steadily gone up. The average person's income has steadily risen. Our spending on luxuries has grown. So has the number of homeless people.

Do homeless people just have bad luck? Should we blame housing that costs too much? Jobs that pay too little? Families less willing or able to help poor relatives? Perhaps the best way to understand why people become homeless today is to listen to their stories.

Even though the United States is one of the richest countries in the world, the number of homeless people is growing.

THE KURTZ FAMILY

Kaitlin Kurtz woke to the sound of a baby crying. She rubbed her tired eyes. Then, out of habit, she reached for the clock on the night table next to her bed. The clock wasn't there. Nor was the night table. Of course! she realized. This wasn't home. This was the Salvation Army shelter.

Katie still couldn't believe it. She sat up on the cot that was now her bed and looked at the rest of her family. Her parents and her two brothers were still asleep. Their cots almost touched her own. Two days ago, she still had had her own bedroom. Two days ago, she had woken to the smell of eggs frying and coffee perking in the kitchen. But even two days ago, life had been different—very different—than it had been for years.

Since Katie was seven, her family had lived in the same apartment. And ever since she could remember, Katie's father had worked at the steel mill that employed most of the men in their Ohio town. Her family wasn't rich, but she got presents for Christmas and pumpkins for Halloween. She had her own bedroom, and her bedspread was her favorite shade of pink.

Life changed shortly after Katie's eleventh birthday. She came home from school to find her father sitting in the kitchen. He had lost his job. He wasn't the only one. Lots of men in town had lost their jobs at the steel mill. Her father said it was a temporary *slowdown*. For a while, the mill would produce less steel and need fewer workers. But eventually production would go back to normal, and he would go back to work.

To make ends meet, Katie's mom took a part-time job at the local grocery store. Katie missed having her home after school every day, but her dad was there. He collected unemployment while he looked for new work. But when the steel mill slowed down, so did work elsewhere. Katie's dad couldn't find a job. He seemed changed. He hardly joked with her anymore. That Christmas, Katie's parents said they couldn't afford a tree.

Katie wished not having a Christmas tree had been the worst that had happened. Six months after her dad lost his job, Katie's family got a letter from their landlord. He had sold the building. They had to move.

Katie's parents looked for a new apartment, but they couldn't find one they could afford. Finally, they put their names on a list of people waiting for low-cost housing. The list was long, too long. They would not get an apartment before they had to move.

Two days ago, Katie packed her pink bedspread into a box. She watched her father put the box into his truck and drive it to her uncle's house for storage. She could have stayed at her uncle's house, but he didn't have room for the whole family. The Kurtzes moved into the shelter.

It was morning now. Katie had to dress for school. She wished someone would stop that baby from crying!

Katie found the suitcase with her clothes. As she dressed, she wondered what she'd tell her friends. How would she explain that she didn't have a phone number anymore?

THE NEW POOR

Kaitlin's family is typical of a new type of homeless. They are working people who lose their jobs and then their homes. They are called the *new poor*.

The new poor may be pushed into poverty when the places they work lay off workers or close. Often, the jobs they lose paid well but did not require formal

Some of the "new poor" are people who have lost their jobs because of factory layoffs or closings. When they can no longer afford their houses or apartments, they become homeless.

training. Many such jobs were found in industries like steel and textiles. Our country has lost two million of these jobs *each year* since 1979. The reason? These industries are dying out in America. In many cases, foreign companies can make the same goods for less money.

Our family farms are also dying. Many farmers took out loans in the late 1970s to buy more land and new equipment. At the time, people thought they would be able to sell a lot of food abroad. This did not happen. In the early 1980s, the sale of farmers' crops began to drop, while the amount of money they had to pay to banks for their loans went up. Many can't pay their debts. So about 2,000 farmers give up farming each week. They, too, are part of the new poor.

Still others among the new poor are divorced women and their children. Many have had to leave husbands who hurt or abused them or their children. Many have never had jobs. They have no job skills or experience. Yet they must support themselves and their families.

Where do these people turn? They could get new jobs to replace those they have lost. But many of these pay poverty-level wages. There are jobs serving hamburgers in fast-food restaurants. There are jobs washing dishes or windows or cars. There are jobs stocking shelves at food stores; aiding teachers at day-care centers; frying doughnuts at coffee shops. They do not pay enough to buy food, clothes, and a home for a family. The new poor can too easily become the new homeless.

Like the Kurtzes, some of the new poor are making ends meet when they are forced out of their homes. Others simply can't pay for their housing. When people can't pay back the money they borrowed to buy their homes, banks *foreclose*, or take over, the houses. When people can't pay the rent, landlords *evict* them, or force them to leave.

Finding a new place to live is a problem for poor people. Low-cost housing is disappearing in our country. This is happening for many reasons. In the 1960s and 1970s, cities started *urban renewal* projects. People tore down block after block of old, low-cost housing to make way for new office buildings. The old apartments were never replaced.

In other places, developers have turned old, low-cost apartments into high-priced ones. Poor people must move out. People with more money move in. When neighborhoods change in this way, it is called *gentrification*. Still other buildings with low-cost apartments have been abandoned or lost to fires.

We have lost about 2.5 million low-cost housing units since 1980. At the same time, the government is not helping as much to build new *public housing*. Public housing is partially paid for by the government, so poor people will have a place to live. In some cities, the wait to get public housing takes years. In New York City, the wait is 18 years.

Many people argue that the answer to homelessness is simple: Create more low-cost housing. For families like

Finding a new place to live is hard for poor people. More and more, inexpensive housing is being replaced by newer, higher-priced housing.

Kaitlin's, that would be the answer. But housing alone won't solve the problem for everyone. Michael's story shows why.

MICHAEL

Michael's hands were cold. They were most cold where they touched the whiskey bottle from which he drank. He didn't care. The whiskey would warm him. The whiskey would make him forget the cold as it made him forget everything else.

Michael sat in the parking lot and leaned against the dumpster. He watched the people in their clean clothes and warm coats walk to their carefully parked cars. He watched them look away as they passed him. They looked away from his filthy, torn army jacket. They looked away from his matted hair, from his face bruised in a fall that morning. Mostly, they looked away from his eyes—blue eyes that stared right at them and dared them to help.

Michael had been like them once. He had had a car and a warm coat and shirts that his wife ironed each week. He had even had a daughter. He was young when she was born, 22. He was young when he left her to serve in the Vietnam War.

Michael was still young when he returned from Vietnam, but he didn't feel it anymore. He didn't feel much of anything except when the flashbacks came. The flashbacks were memories so strong that he thought he was back in the jungle, still fighting the war. He almost killed his daughter during one of those. He thought she was the enemy. After that, he left home.

Michael couldn't remember how long it had been since he'd last seen his daughter. He couldn't remember when he'd given up on making a life for himself and started to drink. Most of the time he didn't want to remember. He drank in order to forget.

Michael rested his head on the cold metal of the dumpster and took another swig of whiskey. The sun was setting. It was getting very cold. He would sleep in the dumpster tonight, he decided. The decaying food would keep him warm.

ALCOHOLISM AND MENTAL ILLNESS

Michael represents the largest number of homeless Americans. More families than any other group become homeless every day. But there are still more homeless single men and women than families. Most of them are men. They are more likely than families to stay homeless.

Like Michael, many homeless men and women have alcohol and mental problems. Over half are addicted to alcohol or other drugs. One-third to one-half have a chronic mental illness. Chronic means that the illness will not go away with time.

Many of those who are mentally ill used to live in big state hospitals. In the 1960s, new drugs were discovered that helped some patients get better. These patients could move back to their communities, although they still needed care.

Many people thought living in their communities was better for patients than living in hospitals. They would have been right, had cities and towns developed enough housing and help for mentally ill people. But they didn't. As a result, many who now need care don't get

Today, there are more homeless single men and women than families.

it. What is more, they cannot work. They cannot keep apartments. They cannot take care of themselves. So they end up on the streets.

Some of the mentally ill homeless are war veterans like Michael. The Veterans Administration (VA) provides free or low-cost health care for veterans such as Michael. But homeless veterans often don't receive this care. One reason is that VA clinics often are located far from where homeless people stay. The American Legion, a veterans' group, says that patients who can get to the clinics don't get enough treatment. They are let out of the hospital before they are well and won't get enough help in the community. In 1986 and 1987, Congress agreed to pay for new programs to help homeless veterans. With luck, they will make a difference.

Health problems make many men and women like Michael homeless. Then there are all the illnesses and injuries that are *caused* by living in shelters or on the street. These afflict all homeless people. Street people who sit or stand all day may have trouble with their feet, legs, or blood flow. They may have skin problems because they cannot protect themselves from the sun, wind, or cold. They may have coughs, colds, or more serious infections. They may freeze. The sad stories of

The stress of being homeless can cause mental problems for many of the people who live on the streets.

homeless people who have frozen to death are reported in newspapers every winter.

Many don't get the minimum amount of food needed for basic good health. Those who live in crowded shelters catch diseases that spread from person to person. Homeless people, especially street people, are often the victims of crime. They are beaten or raped. Says one shelter director, "The question isn't *whether* a homeless woman will be raped, it's *when*."

Homeless people also have a harder time getting medical help. They have no telephones to call the doctor. No cars to drive to the hospital. No refrigerators or kitchen cabinets in which to store medicines. Even if they get help, sometimes they can't do what the doctor says. It's hard to stay warm and get lots of rest if you have no bed. It's hard to stick to a salt-free diet when you can't cook your own food. It's hard to keep your feet up when curbs are your only chairs.

Finally, the stress of being homeless can cause mental problems. What happens to the way people think when they have nowhere to sleep? Can't buy food or warm winter coats? Are cold and sick and can't find help? How do you think they feel?

JENNY

Jenny checked again. She reached deep in the pocket of her faded jeans and felt the folded bill. It was her secret stash—the five dollars she would not spend, no matter how hungry she was. This five was for a real emergency. Hunger was not an emergency. Hunger was just a daily nuisance. She could take care of it. She always did.

Jenny listened to her stomach growl. Okay, okay, she thought. Time to get moving. She stood up and stretched. Her back ached. The backache was becoming as familiar as the hunger pains. She'd slept on the floor again last night, along with the other street kids. She'd met them when she came to San Francisco two weeks before. They called themselves the Street Hawks. They said they had hawks' eyes for spotting empty buildings they could crash in for the night.

The Street Hawks had taught Jenny how to survive on the streets. They showed her the best places to beg for money. They taught her that abandoned buildings were safer to sleep in than subways or parks. Fewer winos and crazies, they said. They taught her that if they stayed together, they were less likely to be beaten or robbed.

This wasn't what Jenny had expected. She had dreamed about leaving home for years. She'd dreamed about it every time her father drank too much and her mother broke into tears. She'd tried a couple of times before. She'd get to the bus terminal, or she'd stay at a friend's for a few nights. But she never made it out of town.

This time was different. She had saved $50, and she

always had the money on her. She had $20 for the bus ticket and $30 to hold her until she got a job. She even had a suitcase packed. It was ready with some sweaters, her favorite albums, an extra pair of jeans. But the last night at home, her father started smashing her mother's favorite china. Jenny didn't stop to take the suitcase. She just ran. In San Francisco, she could start a new life.

She had a new life, all right, but it wasn't the one she had imagined. No one would hire a runaway without an address. Without work she had no money. She still had the five. And the quarters well-dressed commuters dropped in her palm when she begged at the bus station. Once, Jenny had called home. She hung up when she heard her mother's voice. She couldn't talk. She cried instead.

RUNNING TO THE END OF NOWHERE

Runaways like Jenny are only a small part of the homeless population. But their stories are among the most painful. Often, teenagers run away from violent and abusive homes. Less often, they are thrown out by parents who no longer want them.

Not all runaways come from homes this troubled. Some are just having trouble getting along with their parents. They think their parents are too strict. They think life on their own will be easier and more fun. These runaways are more likely to return home. More than a million American teenagers run away each year. Only some of them remain homeless.

Like Jenny, most runaways leave home several times before they end up on the streets of a strange city. And like her, few find the lives they had imagined. Runaways have few job skills and little chance of employment. They learn quickly that life on the streets is rough. They must beg for food money. If they can't get enough, they turn to drugs or prostitution. This often happens within a month of being on the streets, says one person who works with runaways.

The life runaways run to is violent. In 1988, Massachusetts police found the bodies of six murdered prostitutes. A runaway girl from a quiet suburban town was raped and murdered. A New York runaway who committed suicide made the cover of the *New York Times* magazine. More runaways are victims of crimes that don't make headlines but do scar the soul. Says one, "You learn to survive. You also learn not to care if you don't."

Increased risk of illness is another problem for runaways. Both drugs and prostitution carry the risk of *AIDS*, a fatal disease. Drug users can get AIDS from sharing needles. Prostitutes can get it from their sexual partners.

Many cities have special programs to help runaway

teenagers. In Louisville, Kentucky, for example, over 200 stores, fire stations, hospitals, and other places take part in "Project Safe Place." They display yellow stickers in their windows. Teenagers can stop for help at any place with a yellow sticker. People there will put them in touch with volunteers who can arrange shelter or other services. In other cities, *outreach workers* go to places like train and bus stations where runaways hang out. They talk to the teenagers, try to get them to accept help.

These are just some examples of how cities reach out to homeless teenagers. In one sense, many runaways do have homes—their parents' homes. With help from caring adults, they can often return there or find safer places to live.

Most runaways leave home in search of better lives. Many, however, end up living on the streets.

SUNNY, CORRINE, AND CLYDE

Sunny swooped the baby away from the wall, shouting, "No, no, no! Don't eat that!" How could she make him understand? How could she possibly make a 12-month-old infant understand the paint he wanted to eat was dangerous? It contained lead. Lead is poison.

She put the baby down on the bed and looked around the room. The paint was peeling. The radiator hissed steam so hot it could burn. The sooty window had no view. Sunny looked at her daughter, Corrine, who was drawing on the back of a grocery bag. They had no other paper. Corrine looked up from her drawing. "I'll watch Clyde," she said softly. Sunny nodded and sank into the only chair in the room. Then she did what she did most days. She cried.

Sunny had been poor all her life. So had her mother and her grandmother. She grew up in New York City's South Bronx, a violent slum filled with drug dealers and decaying buildings. When she was 17, Corrine was born, and Sunny went on *welfare*. She began getting money from the government to pay for housing and food. It wasn't much, but she lived with her mother and younger brothers. It was okay.

Then someone set fire to their building. Sunny's family moved in with her older sister. Her sister had three children and a one-bedroom apartment. It was too crowded. The kids fought. Sunny and her sister fought. After a month, she moved out.

Sunny and her children lived in shelters for months before the city placed them in the welfare hotel they now called home. It was no home. Every week, Sunny looked for an apartment. It was impossible. Welfare would give her about $250 a month for housing, and the cheapest apartments in New York cost almost $400 a month.

Sunny watched her children playing. Sometimes she dreamed they all lived in a white house. It had window boxes in which she planted red flowers. When her children came home from school, she gave them cookies and helped them with their homework. Sunny wanted that house. She wanted to bake cookies. She wanted a better life for her children. She did not know how to get it.

THE CYCLE OF POVERTY

Most homeless families in large cities are like Sunny's. They are headed by single mothers with two or three young children. Some of these mothers have left husbands who hurt them or their children. Some have divorced for other reasons, only to find they can't support their families. Others, like Sunny, have never been married.

Most of these mothers are in their late 20s. Many had their first children when they were still teenagers. Often, they dropped out of high school. They have no job skills. Even if they did, they would have no one to watch their children if they worked. Since they can't work, they go on welfare.

Welfare is a word people use to describe the money and services our government gives the poor. A homeless mother like Sunny may get money to meet the basic costs of life, plus food stamps and a little money to pay carfare while she looks for housing. The government will pay for her family's health care. It will provide extra money for food if she is pregnant and for each child under five.

Although this sounds like a lot, the actual amount of money is not enough for a family to live on in most cities. Since the early 1970s, costs for food, clothing, and shelter have gone up faster than welfare payments. Welfare mothers can buy less with their benefits today than they could 20 years ago. The amount of money families receive varies from state to state. This is because states pay some and the federal government pays some. In all but three states, benefits are below the poverty level.

The catch is that homeless families have a hard time getting off welfare. If a mother gets a job, she loses her benefits, including housing. Most landlords want two months' rent in advance from new tenants. A woman who has been on welfare and starts a new job doesn't have that kind of money. And, of course, many welfare mothers have few job skills. The jobs they do find pay poorly. They are caught in a *cycle of poverty*.

What can get them off welfare? Job training. Day care for their children. Respectable clothes to wear to work. Food to help them feel and be healthy. Without these things, the door out of the welfare hotel is locked.

COMING IN FROM THE COLD

Kaitlin's, Michael's, Jenny's, and Sunny's stories show that homeless people find places to sleep. Some, like Michael and Jenny, make do on the streets. They sleep in abandoned buildings and sheltered doorways. They sleep in train stations, campgrounds, and cars. They turn dumpsters, steam grates, and cardboard boxes into beds.

Not everyone who is homeless sleeps on the street. Many emergency shelters have opened to provide beds for the homeless. These range from huge, city-run rooms with row after row of cots all the way to church basements with only a few beds. Some are run by groups that have long helped the needy, like the Salvation Army and the Red Cross. Most shelters serve only men or women or families.

This network of shelters has sprung up quickly in response to the homeless crisis. As a result, many shel-

In large cities, shelters for the homeless fill up fast. Many people must continue to sleep outside on the streets.

ters are in places not meant to house people. Some cities have made armories into shelters, for example. Armories are large buildings made to store weapons.

Shelters vary greatly in quality. Some, including many run by private groups, are clean and safe. Others are dirty, overcrowded, and dangerous. People are robbed or beaten. In cities like New York, some shelters are so unsafe that homeless men and women prefer to sleep on the streets. Even many good shelters are in bad neighborhoods.

Some shelters don't have enough toilets or showers.

Some have no kitchens and cannot provide food. Few provide people with privacy. In addition, most shelters give limited help. They are meant to provide a bed for a few nights while someone finds other housing. Many shelters make people leave by six or seven o'clock in the morning. Some will not let someone stay for more than a few nights at a time.

Still, for most homeless people a bed in a shelter is better than no bed. But even a shelter bed isn't always easy to find. Many cities do not have enough shelters to house all of their homeless. For example, Detroit has about 25,000 homeless but only 1,300 shelter beds. Chicago has only 2,800 shelter beds for more than 25,000 homeless. On cold winter nights, they turn people away.

Welfare hotels are another type of housing for homeless people. They serve mothers and children who get financial aid from the government. They offer longer stays than emergency shelters, but they still are only temporary.

Most welfare hotels have only one thing in common with other hotels: they're expensive. The state of Massachusetts, for example, pays over $1,300 a month to keep a family in a welfare hotel. You can rent a *very* nice apartment for that.

Many welfare hotels are old and poorly maintained. Toilets back up and overflow. Radiators break. Old paint peels from grimy walls. Since these are hotels, they do not have room for children to play. Families are crowded into one or two rooms. There are no stoves.

Many rooms do not even have refrigerators. Mothers can't cook for their children. Children go hungry. And as a ten-year-old boy told a group of government officials, "It hurts to be hungry."

HOW WE HELP THE HOMELESS

Many Americans are trying to help the homeless. Our Congress passed a bill that provides money for food, shelter, health care, job training, and schooling for homeless children.

Private citizens and groups help, too. Hundreds of programs for homeless people are run by churches, synagogues, and other private groups. Most people serving meals and working in private shelters are volunteers. Ordinary men and women across the country have given extraordinary help:

• In many cities, private groups and the government work together to help. Thanks to that, in St. Louis any homeless person can get shelter within 24 hours. There is also a day center for mothers and children. The center provides meals, plus practical help, like rides to job interviews and Laundromats.

• A group called Partnership for the Homeless runs shelters in churches and synagogues throughout the country. Volunteers cook and serve meals.

42

• Famous people help, too. People as different as the Reverend Jesse Jackson, Mary Lou Retton, and Bill Cosby joined hands with thousands of other Americans for "Hands Across America." The event raised money for programs that help hungry and homeless Americans.

These are just a few examples. Thousands and thousands of Americans give every day to help homeless people. Their efforts do help.

They don't, however, solve the problem of homelessness. That will take more job training, more services for people with alcohol and mental health problems, and, most of all, more good, low-cost housing.

HOW YOU CAN HELP THE HOMELESS

You can help the homeless, too. Learning about homeless people and their problems is the first step in helping. A problem must be understood before it can be solved.

You can also help by sharing your knowledge. Other people, including many adults, don't know as much about homeless people as you do now. Their false ideas may keep them from helping.

When we help homeless people, we help ourselves. For example, when adults have jobs and houses, they contribute to our society. When children have enough food and go to school every day, they learn skills and ideas valuable to our country.

You can also take action. When Emily's class took a field trip into Chicago, she saw a homeless person begging. She got so upset she decided to do something. She wrote letters to people in power asking their support for programs that help the homeless. She asked her parents and teacher to write, too.

Here are some other ways to take action:

1. Reach out to homeless children; be a pen pal. Many churches, synagogues, and community groups run programs that help homeless families. They might be able to give your letter to a homeless child who needs a friend. Include a stamped return envelope with your letter so your pen pal can write back.

2. Clean out your closet for the homeless. Groups that help homeless people welcome gifts of clothing and toys.

3. Give a gift. Next holiday season, ask your parents to spend some of your gift money on the homeless.

4. Organize a "Help the Homeless Day" at your school. By working together, you and your classmates can give a lot to the homeless. Ask your teacher to help. Name a day as "Help the Homeless Day." You, your classmates, and your teacher can plan ways to help the homeless.

SOME FINAL WORDS

Homelessness in America is already a vast problem, and it could get worse. One report done for Congress said nearly *19 million* Americans could be homeless by the year 2003. You will be old enough to vote and work then. Perhaps you will be living in a nice apartment. Shouldn't everyone be able to do the same?

We are a vast—and rich—nation. We have many resources like food and money to solve the problems of homelessness. We can build or rebuild houses, find people jobs, heal the sick. We have lawmakers who can assure every American a place to live.

Most of all, we have people. No one person can solve the problem of homelessness. But everyone can help.

For Better or For Worse®   **by Lynn Johnston**

FOR MORE INFORMATION

For more information about the homeless, write to:

Child Welfare League of America
440 1st St. NW, Suite 310
Washington, DC 20001

The Coalition for the Homeless
105 East 22nd Street
New York, NY 10010

National Student Campaign Against Hunger
29 Temple Place
Boston, MA 02111

Partnership for the Homeless
6 East 30th Street
New York, NY 10016

GLOSSARY/INDEX

ADDICTION 7, 12, 28 — *A physical need for substances like alcohol or drugs.*

AIDS 34—*A fatal disease caused by a virus found in blood and other body fluids. The virus can be passed from person to person through sexual intercourse or by sharing needles during drug use.*

BARRIO 17—*The Spanish word for an area of a town, often used for slums.*

CYCLE OF POVERTY 37, 39 — *The recurring lack of education, job skills, and money that keeps a family in poverty from one generation to the next.*

DISPLACED WORKERS 11—*People trained to do jobs that no longer exist.*

EVICT 25—*To force people out of their apartments because they can't pay the rent.*

FORECLOSE 25—*To take back a house or farm because the owners can't pay back the money they borrowed to buy it.*

GENTRIFICATION 25—*The moving of middle-class or wealthy people into a renewed city area where poor people used to live.*

MENTAL ILLNESS 7, 8, 12, 28, 29—*One of a number of diseases of the brain that affect a person's thinking and behavior.*

MIGRANT 17, 18—*A person who moves to new cities or towns in search of work.*

GLOSSARY/INDEX